SONGS
of the
SOUL

A Poetic Journey

To my children

May you recognize that which is good
May you touch that which is good
May you become part of that which is good
And may you bring good to that which is

The poet in me
Is not so sure
And so I write
To allure

You away
From your thoughts
To me and mine
And what I caught

Up in my soul
Bearing down my
heart
Please come along
Let us start

To explore this world
Of poems and words
So I can share
A thought I heard

In my mind
That only will rest
If I share it here
For you to test

Don't be afraid
Don't be shy
Let the words sink in
Give it a try

Read and write
Speak and shout
The poem within
Must come out

It is a prayer, you
know
Of course you do
It speaks of its author
This much is true

And then it travels
With just a nod
On the wings of a
word
To you; to God

I now say thank you
To you who read
To those in my poems
And the Creator
indeed

On Being Human

"The planet desperately needs more peacemakers, healers, restorers, storytellers, and lovers of all kinds. It needs people to live well in their places. It needs people with moral courage willing to join the struggle to make the world habitable and humane, and these qualities have little to do with success as our culture defines it." David Orr

You came to me the
other day
From a place I did not
know
My delight at knowing
you were back
Made my heart all
aglow

I missed your soft and
gentle way
I knew when we were
young
And honestly I always
knew
You'd come back and
find my song

But the space was
good; you took your
time
To grow and be
yourself
And when we met
again
We could reach and
be of help

To one another as a
friend

To help us through
this new life
To hold a hand, to
give an ear
And often to give
advice

And now I'm blessed
to have you near
To let you know I care
And as long as you
wish me close by
We'll laugh, cry and
share

So live my friend and
do not be afraid
Of what we may have
lost
There is no loss in
living your life
Only regrets have their
cost

I have none for you
are in my thoughts
Whether close or far
And whether we talk
or take a space
You're forever in my
heart

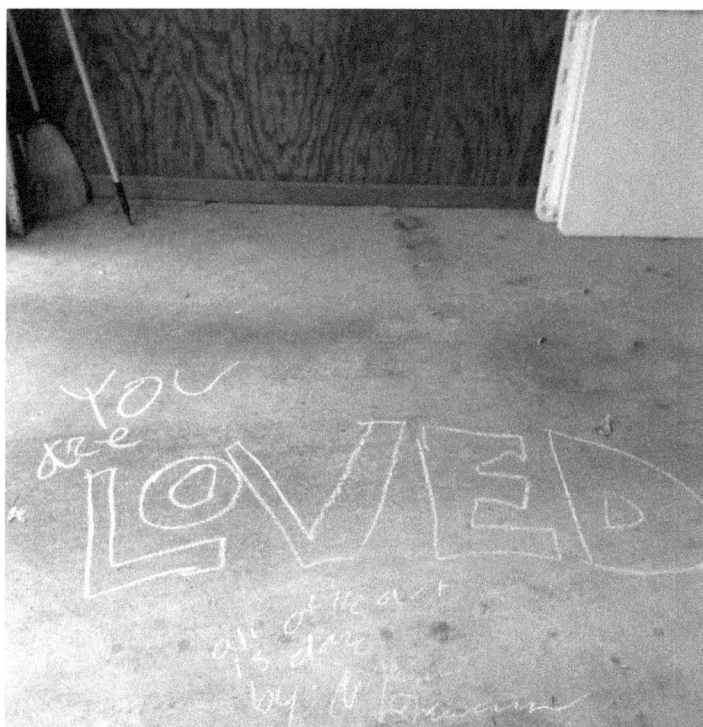

The Feeling abounds
I thought it deep down
Its meaning
Its reason
I know not now
Something missing
Or maybe just found
A smile a glance
So secure and sound
Pitty me not
My life is so rich
Then why always this stirring
Why this itch
The strangeness of it all
Difficult to know
Why you've touched me
And you don't even know

At first glance I did
not know
Why I was there
On this road so many
treaded
And why the impulse
...so unclear

I had so many choices
So why at this spot?
Could He already
know
The purpose I sought?

You stood so strong
A smile...so gentle, so
kind
Your words I took
notice
Their stirring in my
mind

My presence was silent
I knew not what to say

I observed from
distance
To not err...I prayed

Why should I care?
This passing would be
Did I know you
before?
Was all this destined?
For me?

I took from that visit
A lightening in my
heart
For you it seems so
constant
For me...just a start

So I blessed the day
And I started a new
I prayed I would touch
others
As I was touched by
you.

A group of individuals
A sunny autumn day
Colors so bright
The air so clean and crisp
Thoughts shared
Words uttered
Knowledge gained
Sounds of life
Music to our ears
Eyes of love
Experiencing life
Together
One with each other
The spirit of truth

You may have known me
From what you've seen
And I have watched
You and what you've been
A friend that is
A smile
A wink
Each time we met
You gave me something to think
About myself
Or maybe about you
Or life as it goes on
And what may be true
Or how we hurt
Or how we survive
We shared a meal
A laugh or a cry
And words of
Life
Danced on our lips
Crossed our minds
Our ears and hearts
So that I will miss
Sharing this place
We shared for
So long
A serendipitous
Divine song

I've seen you struggle
With your life
It's the same concern
That causes you strife

But stepping away
Is not your way
So you keep at this problem
So that you can stay

But it's not good for you
And it makes you sad
And then there are times
It makes you so mad

And watching it
Has effected me so
You have to see that
I'm just like you, you know

We are stayers we are
You and me
We will sting ourselves
Before we go free

So we stay and we suffer
Banging our heads on the wall
Like Humpty Dumpty
Who had the great fall

Dumb stupid egg
Didn't he care?
Didn't he know?
That eggs don't belong up there?

No one will get you
Out of your spot
And the target of your anger
Is all that you've got

So its best if you
Get up and go
And leave behind
What you had what you know

It's just not good for you
To stay
In a place that causes such pain
When leaving just may

Give you some peace
And let you be you
Without feeling bad
Without feeling blue

Go on, you can do it
Just walk out the door
Pick yourself up
Get up off the floor

There's a new day out there
And you're ready to glow
We're waiting for you
Not get up and go

There is no doubt
I'm sure of it
That we call you dog
It seems to fit

For if we flip
Your name around
It's God we say
And God is found

In your love
That you give away
Unconditionally
Every day

Happy when you walk
Happy when you eat
Happy when you wake
Happy on your feet

Your kisses come
All over my face

Your sweet little body
Your warm embrace

You snuggle and play
You wait and wait
For me to return
Back home each day

Loyalty to all
Who treat you with
love
No doubt you were
sent
From the One above

Such gratitude to you
For being my friend
I'll love you my sweet
one
Until the very end

My furry friend
You light up my life
You just being you
Such sweetness of mine
With skin so soft
And fur so yummy
Your tail tells me all
When your sad, happy or funny
But it's your soul so sweet
That was sent to us all
To rescue us
On days when we fall
How do you do it?
Just being yourself
It takes so little effort
You comfort so well
I often wonder why
We met this time around
And I know that God is just good
And sends his love wrapped up and bound
In the form of a dog
Who knows how to love
Who has stolen our hearts
And was sent from above

Sometimes I share too much
Of me
And you are kind
To be a friend
To receive what I offer
And take it
I reach to you as
Maybe I'm not sure if
I can stand alone
And need a friend to hold
My hand
Two can conquer
More than myself
Alone
So you reach
And we walk the walk
Going where no one's been
But then one day
They call your name
And you let go
Of my hand
And so I'm left
By myself
Standing
All alone
And you walk on
Not looking back
For you have work
To be done
So perhaps I need
To stand
On my own
Alone

I wonder who is in my spot
The one where I used to be
I wonder if they feel my soul
And the space where I was me

I liked my spot where I sat
And had a thought or two
And sometimes I would talk to God
Or fiddle with my shoe

There were other souls who sat nearby
Doing much the same
And it comforted me to know they were there
And that they knew my name

Sometimes we would chat
Me and my soul-sitting friends
But mostly we just sat and thought
Of life from beginning to end

We wondered where we fit
Amongst the world we knew
And how we could live our lives
Better, and what we could do

We listened to words of advice
That came from High and Above
And then we'd wonder if we were
Doing enough, and how to spread the love

But then one day I had to leave
And so I left my spot
And though I moved to somewhere else
A part of me did not

I left a part of myself
Right there in that place
And part of me is still right there
Though you don't see my face

Because where we stop to think
Or spread a thought or two
Leaves a soul print in its place
And gift for the next soul too

Someone else I'm sure is there
Thinking thoughts they could
And I pray what I left behind
Is a blessing that is good

Choice
It must be mine
Not yours
To make for me
I must learn
On my own
The lessons they teach
To find
My own way
To choose
For myself
My will
It's mine
From me
The feeling
Now
Felt by me
You cannot
Decide
The right
And the wrong
But you can love
The Me
I become

You called me the other day
Just to say hello
And though I thought you didn't care
There was so much I didn't know

Like how bad you felt
When they sent me away
And how you just wanted to talk
And that you wanted to pray

That I'd stay around
And in your voice
I'd be pleased you called
I had no other choice

But to hug you from my place of sad
To hear how much you care
About the loss to my heart
And thoughts I could not share

I'll miss the time and space we shared
We made such a great team
And knowing you've got my back
Will help me continue to dream

And do what I love to do
And use the gifts I was given
To help others live their best
To help others be driven

So thank you my dear friend
For being brave and bold
For calling to let me know you're here
A friendship made of gold

The most precious of gifts are intangible and unexpected, often unnoticed. Sometimes we awaken years later only to realize what was bestowed upon us. Often we might mistake its contents buried in a physical pleasure, but the real gift is the message left behind.

To fly
To live
Each of you a wing
The wind is your life
The earth is your home
Your eyes are windows
Two souls from a source
One wing will rest
The other will turn
From different directions
Our world is learned
When wings are worn
Feet will hold
When hearts direct
Minds will know
The flight you embark upon
To where no one's ever flown

Your sweet old face
Tells it all
A tall tale it tells
Of your song and call
And your advice to me
Wear lipstick?
Really?
Is that what you
learned?
I suppose that is
plenty
For in my face you
See future years
Go out and grab them
Is your cheer
For me
For you say
You are near the end
And so you want me
To go on as your
friend
My life you see
The future is bright

You think I'm so
young
But where is your
light?
I see it you know
You're not done yet
And beside, that soul
You bare must know
It's just beginning its
journey
And so
The lipstick my friend
Is not just for me
But for your lips as
well
Yes, at 103
At which point a kiss
Will form on your
face
To wave you on
From this most
awesome place
To the rest of your
journey
And we will meet
again
For my lipstick friend
This is no end

They say you're
different
That's true
Than what?
Than her?
Than him?
Then what we
expected
You to be?
So what?
If it's true?
Does that make me
Less than you?
Not a fit
For what you
Thought I'd be?
Or you're too good
For what I see?
Or just too strange
So that I'm not sure
If others will make
An opinion
A cure?

Like you need that?
I don't think so
Perhaps they need
To adjust
And flow
With who you are
And what I am
How dare they
Question
The Divine plan
That loves us all
For who we are
And embraces
Each one
Near or far
Color or race
Religion or country
Ability or challenge
We come from
An infinite bowl
Of light
Living together
Is simply
Right

Hello there mat
We meet on the floor
With others who
practice
Will walk through the
door

But this space I've
chosen
Is just for us
You are my ground
And it's you that I
trust

To provide a base
A place where I'll
move
Or be very still
Please don't
disapprove

Somethings we will do
With ease and so
smooth
Some moves so hard
But I'll breathe
through those too

And what I do on my
mat

Is for me alone
Though others silently
Will be cheering me
on

As they too will be
breathing
Holding and moving
Stretching and
reaching
A practice so soothing

And I'll take what I
learn
To the rest of my
living
To be present to be
open
To be strong and
giving

But it's you my mat
Who has become my
good friend
You're always
underneath
Until the very end

27

When I roll you up
And take you along
For you never leave
your mat
That would be wrong

And any practice
Has something that
we use
To keep us in focus

To help us get
through

And if we are better
For having taken the
time
I'll say, Thank you,
God
For this mat that is
mine

Hey, you left your
junk
Right in my lap
That garbage that flew
While taking my nap

I was dreaming of
dogs
And feeling the love
I was walking the
beach
I saw a pure white
dove

Then I woke up and
You dumped all your
crap
Edging God Out
Your EGO right in my
lap

Come pick up your
filth
That's what I should
say
What are you fussing
about?
What ruined your
day?

You silly sweet soul
Did you need some
attention?

While I fell asleep
Were you put in
detention?

It's okay, there now
Just calm down and
rest
Lay your head on my
lap
I'll take care of the
rest

I suppose I forgot
To give you all of my
heart
So my head nodded
off
Not a great way to
start

A conversation you
say
I must really attend
To what you are
saying
And listen to the end

I will try my best
But you don't have to
yell
Just let me know
You're not the guard
to hell

29

Lighten up my loved
one
For even when I'm
asleep
You have all of my
heart
I'm your lost little
sheep

That will follow you
where
Ever you lead
And provide you with
my love
And all that you need

When we look into someone's eyes and we recognize what we see, that is we see a part of God that is ourselves, then we feel a connection, a desire... love. Often we recognize the other person or sometimes we don't recognize anything. But when we feel a pull or recognition, it is a reflection of our own soul that looks back at us.

Perhaps I've had it wrong
I've missed the point all along
That you are here for me
And I for you
Not to take
Or question or ask
To give and give
As long as you want
Or need
Or plea
Or silently beg
Or quietly wait
For me to see
That my only
Task is to honor you
It may be hard
It may be amazing
It may take time
It may make me crazy
But here
Right now
Is what I do
This most honorable task
To honor you

We're glued together
You and I
So much history
Can explain why

And so often
You thought to leave
To go
To fly
To be
Who you are
Or what you saw
You waited from
Near and far

But we didn't go
That's not what we do
We stay. We're like
That monkey glue

That leaves a glob
Near every break
So you remember
What's at stake

Some will go
And create new ways
Their journeys so
colorful
The years, the days

And our takes work
That much is true
But how do you drop
an
Arm that's a part of
you

It hurts sometimes
That broken limb
But it is yours
You're a part of him

So you find what's
good
And you give a smile
A kiss a hug
Embrace for a while

And then you look
back
At all that glue
And you're so glad
He's a part of you

Wing of mine
Side of me
Soaring high
Distant and free
I, earth grounded
For each good-bye
Steady and strong
A tear in my eye
The sky...your home
The ground, just a pause
So risky each trip
Life...your cause
Your final trip
Journey home
Fly high...Fly free
Destination unknown

The other day I made
you mad
When I stopped in
front of you
At a light you wanted
To go on through

So angry you were
I saw you say
Though I could not
hear
I ruined your day

And it made me
wonder
How often it's true
Every decision we
make
Affects someone else
too

A stranger, a friend or
even
Someone we don't
know
Across the great blue
We do something and
so

We don't stop to
think
What we did and how
it made
Someone else feel
Perhaps on a much
later day

We are all part of one
On a large existential
web
And if I pull on my
string
The entire system will
flow and ebb

So if you live on a
mountain top
In a city or in jail
If you serve your
country
A gang or the boat you
sail

If you are right
As you always are
And I am wrong
You'll take your
indignation oh so far

We are all part of
another
One humanity we are
And until we realize
we're on the same ship
We cannot go very far

Pain and anger can
make our vessel
So heavy it may sink
With all of us aboard
From my trying to
make you think

About me and mine
And who I am
About what I need
Move over now Sam!

But if I see you
And you see me
Then we can live and
love
In peace, in life and
harmony

Perhaps the most
difficult word is
No
And not the no with
anger
But the no with
kindness

The no with anger
comes
From the ego
And it hides behind
The rage

But the no with
kindness
Is firm and
Connected to a much
Stronger source

No in this case means
This is not good for
me
This is not ultimately
good

For you

This may hurt me to
say
And hurt you to hear
But will ultimately be
Better for both

This no is the scariest
Most difficult word
I know and it sits
below
My throat

But when I say it
I know its right
And I know I owe no
one
Explanations

It's a loving no
A kind no
A simple no
It's God saying no

I think that all each of us ever desires is for someone to "know" us and to sense and feel that knowing. Perhaps we confuse people by not always being ourselves or perhaps sometimes we, ourselves, are not sure who we are. But when we get a glimpse of ourselves in a quiet unadulterated moment, we feel so completely whole, whether someone else knows us or not. With every significant encounter we meet a new lesson and whether we learn from it, determines whether it becomes a part of ourself that we know.

What purpose is there in loving you?
If not for the growth of your soul?
What purpose has time had in directing us
In growing from young to old?
Do we meet each lifetime
With a purpose on hand?
Or are the shadows we face
The realities we stand?
I have to believe
That to truly live life
We have to touch souls
And awaken them inside
Sometimes we hide
Behind a fear that we face
But deep within
A soul is in place
Whether you can reach me
Or I can touch you
Is the challenge we face
Each day a new
And with each life
Our souls grow stronger
And perhaps with each meeting
Our souls connect longer
But you can be sure
That in this life...my goal
Is to move you in a way
Recognizable ...to your soul

If my worth is determined
By your rightness
Than I must agree
With you and confess

That what you think
And what's in your sight
And what you hear
Is exactly right

And if your worth is
Made by how sure
You are then what I think
Is quite a blur

And has taken a back seat
To make quite sure
That I always agree
And not to stir

The way you think
But to say yes
Even though inside
I'm forming a guess

And wondering if
It's really true
For me that is
And not just for you

As I believe that
Our truths can both exist

Like after a rain when the earth
Fills with both sun and mist

There's room for all thoughts
And ours may differ
But that doesn't mean you
Nor I should have to suffer

For we are worthy
And truly loved
Not just by each other
But from God above

So if you're feeling scared
And perhaps unsure
Please try to remember
That is only your

Little self who's yelling
I am right
Your soul knows better
Never a fight

Your little self
Will be Okay
Just give it a hug
And put it away

Let your love shine through
And reach out to me
For that's whom I know
You to really be

Like the heart beat
She lives
Steady and strong
Keeping in rhythm
To her drummer's drum
She feeds his soul
Sanded in his beat
With a distance
To encourage
The tapping of his feet
Their days grow younger
With simplicity
Honest, love
A witness to truth
Each day is theirs
Each moment a gift
Fear left behind
Now the joy of youth

She wanted to love
Just like you and me
But she came with a
soul
So confused you see

Of what was real
And what is true
And so her heart went
after
The wrong love so
blue

Though her head
knew better
Her heart knew wrong
And it sang of another
A bittersweet love
song

For he belonged to
another
That much she could
see
But she couldn't
understand
Could not believe

That feeling for him

Was wrong no way
Why would she feel?
For another this way?

So she spent her life
Making life work
A poor confused soul
She was the real jerk

Not nice to those
Who were near her so
Who tried to love her
With her heart on her
beau

For what was in front
Was the one she was
given and needed
And he loved her so
He begged and
pleaded

How do we choose
love?
Or does love choose
us?
And can we direct a
heart?
To steer the love bus?

We all know a Scarlet
It might be someone
you see
Who loves their Tara
More than he

And spends their life
Chasing what is not
avail
And misses Clark
Gable
With her head on the
trail

After another or
After the land
Or after money
A hard life and

When she woke up
It was just too late
And so many paid the
price
So much was at stake

And she ran to him
And shouted: I love
you too
But his reply: I don't
give a damn

Was all that was true

Her love was now
Gone with the wind
But she had her land
Perhaps she won in
the end?

You can go after your
love
But if its not there
It's not meant for you
With your head in the
air

Love what you have
For that is all that is
true
It is what is yours right
now
That is all you can do

Love with all your
might
Be the best that you
may
Give to your love with
your heart
For tomorrow's
another day

Shelter me please
Beneath your wings
Provide for me
A moment of peace
A place where I am safe to be
Just me
The one you know and see
Comfort me
When I am down
Tell me that
You'll stay around
Not to push
And not to tease
But to be the shelter
I so desperately need
And when I'm strong
Ready for flight
Step back and watch
Your presence just right
You need not fear
I won't go far from the nest
But, we all need to fly
And have shelter to rest

He loved her once
That much I know
The way he talked
About her lovely glow

And she loved him
That much she knew
He was her beau
And she his true

Love that is
But love can change
From ease and care
To hurt and pain

As life brings strife
So our worst is shown
For those who stay
Versus those who've
flown

So sometimes we live
In another's view
And they never see
The real true you

Because every time
The pattern plays
And the response is
the same

It's the only way

We know how to
respond
Until the day we die
It's the dance of the
enabler
And the addicts reply

So the only way
May be to go
But you will still have
to learn
To live and so

You must turn
yourself
To God above
Only faith can help
Us deal with love

No matter its form
No matter is look
Your love one is
destined
And in the Book

Of life and love
And that is true
But how you reply
Is up to you

The Road Left Behind
Your view so different than mine
Empathy is all mine can be for you
I cannot feel the road
So difficult for me to keep up
To stay
Jumping through hoops
My feet never touching down
Following your map you call divine
Yet my road had no direction
So we left it far behind
Yet I wonder where it went
Maybe my avoiding it not so divine
So where are you going?
When you get there
Will I be left behind?
And all the time
The sacrifice so great
For the road I left behind

Living
With a conscious effort
To connect
To a higher source
Our paths linked together
Destinies unknown
Yours I must accept
Mine you do not own
Cover me
Contain me
Direct me
Destroy me
Yet like a tree
Grows its own way
That bends
Only with the strongest of wind
Or ice...holds firm and then
Very slowly
...it melts
Losing its beauty, purpose and form
From the intimidating warm
Yet I am who I am
Deeper than skin
See me
Hear me
Love me
Know me
Then my life...will begin

I didn't save you
You were afraid
I wasn't strong
I could not see
To leave
To go
To run
So you could be
And not have the
need
To be the one
Protecting me
I too was young
And stuck in a mess
Of adults who wined
and moaned
Not knowing what was
best

We stayed
We stood
We stuck
Like glue
Good or bad
You and me
Some will run
Some will stay
The life you choose
Is the one you made
But those who go
Find what's new
And those who stay
Find the glue
That's how it is
Good or bad
God lets us choose
So don't be sad
You can change
Or you can stay
Draw your sword
Make today your day

I haven't seen you
In a while
But you saw me now
And I your smile

A warm embrace
A hug
A heart
That crosses time
And miles apart

So much to say
To share
To hear
A moment now
Covers every year

Because love is wide
It knows no bounds
A reunion of hearts
Souls and sounds

So grateful you
And I are kin
People who share
A destiny, a win

But aren't we all
Related to another?
And share in this
Life together?

A precious moment
A seed of time
I will treasure this visit
It's yours and mine

And I take with me
The blink of an eye
A gift to see you
And for now goodbye

I wish for you someone kind
To help you through your days
I wish for you someone sweet
To love your every way

I pray for you to be
That person to someone new
I pray that you will be your best
To someone who needs you too

Your higher self will connect
When you meet the person who's right
But only if your lower self
Your ego is out of sight

It may take some work to undo
All the residual pain
That growing often leaves
Like a field soaked in rain

But the sun will shine on you
You only have to know
That it is your soul that now must meet
Your intended when they show

Look for someone who is raw
Honest, good and kind
Look for someone who gives
When no one is looking from behind

Be sure they are real

And value what is true
Be sure their things of worth
Are not tangible but things you do

Be the person you want to meet
Be kind, be thoughtful and giving
Life is not meant for those who are shy
But by those bold enough for living

Hello quiet boy
Are you okay?
Are you deep in
thought?
Would you like to
play?
I miss those days
When life was carefree
You'd romp and run
And giggle with me
But now you're feeling
That itch that comes
From others expecting
Like a beating drum
And you're not so sure
Of who you are
Though I know the
journey
Seems so far
And hard
And frightening
Perhaps even too
much
And maybe the
foundation

Wasn't such
To give you the
footing
That others may have
But your feet are
strong
So take a step
Just try one thing
Don't look back
You can do it
Out of the tunnel you
go
There's light out there
Go on an so
I'll be watching
And waiting to hear
How you found your
place
Go on my dear
Sweet kind boy
Soul I bore
You can do this now
Fly away
Soar

What's my purpose
mom? She asked
Like I should really
know
And if I even did
I'd dare not try to
show
Her what her purpose
is
Because then it's not
really hers
But my interpretation
Of a life
That came through
Me but not
To be
For me to see
Just a bit
Or maybe a lot
But either way
It's hers and I'm not
The director
Of my child's destiny

Just a cheerleader
And supporter
Of what she might be
Or already is
Yes that is her
Key
To just be
With gratitude
To breath
And let others know
How grateful you are
Just let it show
Just let it grow
And so you know
You are God's child
Perfectly imperfect
Here for a while
Not to perfect
But to shine and glow
So fly my bird
Don't sit for too long
The world is your
home
Now sing us your song

I saw your face
Just the other day
It said so much
Your quiet in my way

I noticed how you thought
As I've done so well
But you said not
Of what you felt

So you like me
We ignore that feeling
Deep down inside
Though often reeling

With angst, concern
And even with love
But we keep it deep down
Though it's known from above

Where all thoughts go
And all is known
But it's here to learn
To let them show

So we can grow and learn
And let our self shine
So we can fully comprehend
What is you and mine

Sometime in our youth
We hold back our own light
Sometime in our youth
The quiet becomes right

As those who know us
Tell us we're wrong
Or hurt or push
Killing our song

But I know you're in there
And your song has a voice
I'm just waiting to hear
It is always your choice

To keep inside
What God gave you to share
Or let it spring forth
Let your soul be bare

And show us all
The divine within
Let it sing its own song
And then your life will begin

Little drummer with a beat
Of your own
They keep telling you to beat this and that way
For your rhythms not known
It leads you alone
You must follow it
And call it your own
Let the rhythm guide you
To places on high
May you do wondrous wonders
From the beating rhythm inside

My little one
So petite so small
Full of life
You're on your way
To more than I
I feel the pull
I wipe a tear away
So sweet
So brave
Missing you now
Good luck little one
With love
Forever and now

Heart of mine
The gift of a soul
The true taste of life
Watching a young vine grow bold

My life came apparent
My purpose then told
As changes took place
Rewards took a hold

My wishes for you...
To grow to be kind
To be proud of your image
To voice "it is mine!"

Dream high...dream large
The tools, I provide
Choices abound
Right ones don't hide

Let your minds direct
THE words are so clear
Then your hearts will know
What's right will be near

Our days always in question
So live and play with them well
That when you look back
Only dignity will tell

I didn't know
That you could be
Your best without
A part of me

I thought you had
To have my soul
As it was lost
And yours was whole

Though you were young
And I was older
Yours I could touch
Yours had wonder

So I pushed and molded
Yours to be
Just like mine
Just like me

What I thought was important
What I saw was right
I made you see
Cause I was right

But now you're lost
Just like me
Your soul is buried
Underneath

But I promise you
That it is there
When you were younger
Your soul could bare

All that was beautiful
All that was pure
It's there I know
I'm absolutely sure

All you have to do
Is let it be
All you have to do
Is let go of me

And when you find
Another soul to protect
Let it be
Don't redirect

And it will shine
And it will grow
Simply from
The Love you show

She said she just
wanted
To see him smile
Even though she knew
It might be a long
while

Like other moms
She has hopes it seems
That David would
laugh
Learn and dream

But David cannot
At least not now
Though mom will
never give up
And doesn't know
how

To reach David
She knows he's in
there
Behind the confusion
And sweet tousled
hair

She'd love to
complain
That he dropped her
best vase
Or watch him play
sports
Slide into first base

David can't eat
Without help you see
He doesn't respond to
Mom, Dad or me

But he is surrounded
by love
That much is true
And David came here
To teach me and you

That life is not about
Having or doing
It's much more about
Loving and being

And David we know
You are in your own
space
Singing a sweet song
And a smile on your
face

Stand Tall
Head high
Feet firm
Your colors so clear
Today is your day
Only perspective is behind
Let go of your tears
A million moments more
Your mind may know
Only if your heart is smart
Be kind to all
Be your best...

I never got a chance to meet you
But you were hers
and ours
And so I love you
From here
While you are there
I won't hold you
Or take you for a stroll
Or buy you a toy
Or watch you grow
But I'll always know you
Came to say hi
To teach us
To be
Better Inside
We will meet again
Somewhere else I suppose
And I will know
Who you are
By the love in your soul

What was good for us
But not for them
How do you see?
When you hold a
gem?

To keep it in a box
It will be safe
But cannot sparkle
In such a dark place

You must take it out
And give it light
And let it sine
Its very own bright

But if you use it
For yourself
Then it simply will sit
Up on a shelf

And you may wonder
Why it's dim
Or why it's lonely
A thought of him?

It's OK
You didn't know
You weren't aware
Of the inner glow

So now open the box
And let it out
Let your diamond
glisten
Without a doubt

It's a part of you
Can't you see
Trust it to shine
Just let it be

For when you do
Then you will feel
The love that comes
The one that's real

It is nice to see
That what you've
grown
Has blossomed so well
And is proud to be
shown

And so like many
I'm watching you
And watching others
To see what they do

And how they earn
And how they live
And how they grow
And how they give

Which makes me
wonder
If I'm up to par
Perhaps I'm in need
Of a brand new car

Though that's not
really
My way or care
But I do worry
endlessly
About my children
and their

Choices they make
Or the ones they
cannot

And how I'm to blame
For decisions I
brought

To them when they
were
Young and so small
Did I choose the right
school?
Will they make it? Or
fall?

Of course they will fall
Each and everyone
does
But will they be
strong?
And I wonder because

Everyone else seems so
Strong and a smile on
their look
Or do you think all of
this
Is just on Facebook?

If someone's child
Has a great career
Or just got engaged
Or got 500 likes and a
cheer

Does that make our
lives

On the wrong track?
Is their good my bad?
Their decisions my
lack?

Maybe I need
To see what I have?
And not what I'm not
Now things don't
seem so bad

You're good is yours
And mine is good too
Though my kid may
choose
To shine someone's
shoe

And yours may go to
Medical school
And have 7 children
Or be someone's fool

We just don't know
How this all will turn
out
So best to look in

And learn not to pout

In fact I won't dare
blame
Myself for what I see
God put it in front
To see whom I'd be

Silly and jealous
Or grateful and strong
I'm going with the
latter
Gonna sing my own
song

And all our kids are
amazing
Complicated, simple
or pure
And no matter what
They're loved for sure

They may go or stay
They may work or play
But I know for sure
They will find their
way

I think you may be
The most beautiful person I know
You're raw and pure and I love you
That much I surely know

You were born so perfect
Like an angel with a bow
And everyday has been a privilege
Just to watch you grow

Now your grown and I am in awe
Of the person that you are
And like a butterfly you flew
And landed oh so far

Away from me but then I knew
I had done my job just right
For if you fly and touch others
It means your life took flight

But now and then I get to visit
And you let me have a peek
Of what you do and how you live
Such a blessed treat

We raise our young to leave the nest
That is why we're here
They come through us but are not us
Though we'd love to keep them near

So fly my child you've done so well
Keep going to places unknown
And I'll be watching you always
From this place called home

Hello my son, I'm
going to be fine
Your ship is sailing
now
Don't you see its
flashing light?
It's waiting for you to
come out

Why are you waiting
in your room?
What are you doing
here?
I too would love for
you to stay
But destiny is calling
you there

Your childhood
wounds
Cannot be healed
waiting for a sign
You must go on and
get on that ship
It's your journey now,
not mine

I know you must be
afraid
Perhaps we clipped
your wings

But your feet work
just fine
And you can do all
sorts of things

Don't worry about
what you don't know
No one knows it all
Intelligence is in many
forms
And everyone must
fall

The world is one big
universe
You will learn every
day
That it is a sense of
wonder
That will reward you
and pay

You think you don't
have what it takes
To make it really big
That is not the right
attitude
But you must start
small and start to dig

Out of the hole you
think is safe
Out of the world you
know
The rest of it needs
you now
And God expects you
to show

Up, and out it's time
to move
To take a leap of faith
You will be better
than fine, so pack it
up
I love you, get going
today

Journey in the Dark

"Even in darkness, it is possible to create light"
Elie Weisel

I am not at ease with a definition of roles where the growth of one soul is more important than that of another. By definition, that seems ludicrous, yet by practice it is a reality. And to justify it by lauding the importance of each role is only self-serving. One's requirements should not be used as justification for another's servitude. The path for one particular soul is not necessarily food or fuel for both. The only real soul growth comes from acceptance. Giving must be unconditional with no preconceived ideas of how another's soul should grow.

I don't think anything stings more than rejection
It goes against our own belief of ourselves
So then we question
Who we are
Whether we deserve
To be
To live
A rejection is always personal
There is no such thing as one that is not
And though from the rejecters point of view
It may be necessary
From the rejected
It is always not
It is always personal
It says
YOU
Are not wanted
Are not needed
And then you find yourself
In a place
Afraid to move
Afraid of rejection again
Until you realize
That life may just be
A series of lessons
Most of which come
From rejections
That say
Back up. Wrong Way. Detour. Do not Enter
RECALCULATING
And so you try again

Ugh it eats at my heart
And keeps my mind
racing
And like a yoyo, my
brain
Continues endless
pacing

That you have what I
had
And what I thought
was mine
You stepped into my
life
And now you're the
one that shines

I run it around and
around
How I fell behind
And let you step
ahead
I can't get this out of
my mind

This horrible feeling
of jealousy
Has taken over my
thoughts

And wraps my heart
and brain
In handcuffs that I
bought

For I know that I put
them
Around my own
thinking
And as long as my
mind watches you
I feel like I'm sinking

Jealousy just sucks
And top it with
betrayal
Perhaps I need to
evaluate this lesson
And why I'm on this
trail

For I don't want to
feel
Anything but love
But something had to
be learned
From the One above

Though it feels as if I
will never

Be ever to let this go
I must somehow move
my thoughts
From the past to the
forward and go

To somewhere new
and fresh
Perhaps it's not even a
place
But a new way of
seeing this journey
And my role in the
human race

So the time will come
I pray
When I will bless you
and what you do
I'm asking God to
help me
So I can start anew

For now I'm going to
try
And look forward and
not back
And forgive me but I
need some space
While I get back on
my track

It hurts
This knowing of me
The part I did not
Want you to see

But your fear
Led you to uncover it
Your need to expose me and mine
Bit by bit

Until there was nothing left
For you to see
Except yourself
Inside of me

And that you did not
Like at all
Your reflection Your ego
Looking back

You thought it was me
But you are wrong
It was you
You found all along

Your reactions to what
You heard was done
I'm realizing had so
Little to do

With what he did
Or who she is
But so much more
About you

Your ability
To take your grief
And find a target
To blame

Is quite skillful
I must say
And gives a face
To your internal pain

You run around
Talking and blaming
Someone you hardly
Knew

For this gave a place
For all that yuck
The nasty inside of
You

Honestly you need

Help and stop talking
About how
You love

Don't blow me
A kiss or toss me a
hug
Until you get help
From above

You really are ill
And in denial
Be careful of
What you do

So that finger you are
Pointing at someone
has
Four pointing
At you

Blame is just
So wasteful and only
Serves a
Blow

And gives way
Too much attention
To your Self, a
massage for your
Bruised Ego

So maybe next time
You want to help
Try to stretch your
heart and
Bend

You will try reaching
Out and engaging
Now, that is real love
My friend

The memory
Causes pain
As I recall
Your faces
Your joy
What I thought
Was real
But it was
Not so
At least not
Meant for long
Though I wish
It had been
So deep
And real
We worked
So hard
We changed

To be
We reached
To see
We tried
And tried
And then
It was
Simply
No more
In place
Was something
I did not like
Dark
Alone
Lost
Your face
Your smile
Those were
Gone
In place
Was nothing
I ever knew

It's not so much what
you say
That I hear so loud
But what you don't
Amongst the verbal
crowd

For what you said
You wanted me to
hear
But what you held
back
You did so with fear

But I heard it in the
pause
I heard it anyway
Amongst the silence
In your tone and your
gaze

In fact the words you
did not say
That you held back
Were louder than
The rest of the pack

They landed in
The world that is
hidden

They are still there
Where nothing is
forbidden

And all is known
Your words are
waiting
When we leave this
place
They'll be there saying

What our thoughts
are now
Those that hurt and
those dear
In the world to be
Are heard and clear

So if you must
Please say it out loud
We can then know
the truth
We can figure out
how

To deal with you
To understand me
To be upfront
The life of honesty

While U'r here you might as well make the best of it
— Mike R.

You blocked me out
That's not love
It's your lower self
Not from above

Blocks and bans
Shuts the door
Throws out the key
Not a friend anymore

I don't think
You are so nice
Did you forget I helped you?
This feels like ice

Cold and hard
Mean and cruel
But guess what little one
I'm no fool

I got your number
You smile outside
But inside you're sad
That's where you hide

Silly little girl
Your time will come
You will wonder why
You've been blocked from someone

It's the way the world works
An eye for an eye
God makes it all fair
From way up high

Wishing you the best
Wishing you to be whole
When you unblock your heart
And open your soul

And I won't be waiting
I'm moving along
But I will always love you
That's my soul song

You walked into the party
And avoided me so
Yet you had caused so much pain
This we both know

Sometimes I wish you knew
How much damage you had done
To me and all I love
The battle you thought you'd won

But I decided I could never explain
It all in a way you'd see
And so avoiding your gaze
Was only hurting me

So I approached you with caution
And wished you well with a smile
You wished me the same
And if felt normal for a while

I'll never understand
Why you needed such control
But I'm moving on now
It's much better for my soul

I'll see you now and then
We'll wave and say hello
And then part our ways
Friends again? I'm sorry but no.

For a friend is someone you trust

To help you when you're happy or hurt
A friend will never betray
Or sling a fistful of dirt

But I can wish you well
And give you a kind look
I hope you understand
Trust is something you took

So carry on with life
I'll see you one day again
Where souls are without hurt
And everyone is a real friend

I saw the best you are
And went to bat for you
I put my job on the line
To voice what I knew was true

I thought they might not believe
For they could not see
The best of you that I knew for sure
That you could surely be

And so they finally caved
And let you join the team
We worked so hard to help them grow
We created and built their dream

Then one day without much notice
They grew too fast too big
And so they had to place that stress
On the one who is soft, who gives

I was chosen to have to go
It did not seem too fair
And I looked to you to stand up for me
I wondered, would you dare

But you were quiet as you did fear
That you could sure be next
You stood by and watched me fall
For fear can be quite complex

So I left you in the place I loved

To carry on alone
And I went out into the world
To find the great unknown

It is not what we do I've found
That makes us who we are
It's the courage to be there for others
That will take us to our star

So maybe next time, you will stand
Up, and be a friend
Though perhaps I would have done the same
We won't know until our end

And I have learned too
That when we extend a hand
We do it for the highest good
And expect nothing of this grand

Gesture that comes from the heart
We have a lot to learn
Of how to give and how to live
And with gratitude, character is earned

It may be our best teacher
That moment with a heavy load
Like a flash of light it reveals our selves
When we've turned down our darkest road
It shows us the way back home
Though we may chance closing our eyes to it
We bury it down beneath our soul
Testing our strength and true spirit
But at the most pristine moment
It chooses to reveal its power
It comes as a master teacher
It shines at our darkest hour
And from the cruelest moments
It shows us our true duty
Like the color of our eye that does not see
But shows others our God-given beauty
As we live this life where we stumble and err
We earn our scars for life
And that master teacher that showed us the way?
Shame is the name of that incredible ride

Soul school started
yesterday
But I was late
Finding my way
Is such my fate

I stopped to feel sorry
For another mishap
Mistake and
misdirection
Lost in my SELF trap

I then had to wash
My tears
And mull through
All those wasted years

I had to find
The blame
And figure out why I
have

Such shame

And then I needed
To find my truth
But so many lies
Dating back to my
youth

And so many to ask
For forgiving
That is how I've
Been living

So I'm sorry if
I missed the date
But I showed up now
I hope not to late

So soul school will
Start today
I'm ready now
Let's start, Okay?

It's not what happens to us that matters so much as it is how we respond that draws us closer to our intended path and creates character. When something seems difficult, it is only a challenge beckoning creativity.

To be God-like, we must be creative.

There is no place or time that has a need for passivity or a free ride. Every moment, job, rejection, opportunity, birth, meeting, experience or disaster has within itself the opportunity to be creative. And, if we get bogged down in details of why, we lose the opportunity at hand. When we create we have the opportunity to be bigger than our current self and to expand ourselves to heaven. We can create at any moment in any given situation and circumstance. When we do so with awareness that we are part of a larger process, then we begin to possess the ability to be creative in all aspects of our lives and reach out to those around us. There are then no impossibilities for any moment. There are only choices. Creativity leads to an endless array of choices and then we must face the truth as to whether we are strong enough to act upon them. Creativity brings us closer to free choice, closer to truth and closer to God.

God you scared me the other day
When the opportunity arose
To step out of my comfort zone
So I offered someone else and they chose

I offered her up like a sacrifice
My inadequacy said I could not
But then the light went from me to her
She took that open spot

Our greatest fear is not
What we cannot do
Our greatest fear is our power
Something bold, beautiful and new

We know our story and so we say
This is who we are
But if we don't step out of our skin
We can't go very far

And the story seems to repeat itself
Over and over again
We give up what appears too hard
Though we are capable to win

To be the best of ourselves
To reach until the sky
This is something we can do now and always
Until the day we die

So when you're asked if you can do
Something you've never done
Just say, not now, but I have the internal
Drive to reach unto the sun

Go on, step out on a limb
The universe is waiting, it is yours
God is always by your side
Your power is beyond measure

He loves me. He loves me not. If you know that God loves you, then your self worth will never be based on how much people love you, or what they think of you. You will not do things to hurt yourself or others. The fear of religion will be gone. The fear of change will be gone. The fear of challenge will be gone. However, if you are not sure if God loves you or if you've never or seldom given any thought to it, then who you are will always be defined by external forces and opinions. You will do things, almost anything, to seek approval from others or for physical satisfaction. You will act from a place of fear. Self-esteem and confidence are directly related to your perception of God's love.

Why did she do it?
What happened that day?
She crossed a line
She had to pay

I don't know you
And you don't know me
But I also had a day
That no one would see

But they caught her
And said she was bad
And for that one impulsive act
She'd forever be sad

Do people believe in
A second chance?
A third or fourth?
Not even a glance?

But doesn't every soul
Need a chance to try?
Does hurting a soul
Help the injured get by?

Does the system work
Where you pay for your sin?
Wouldn't love work better
For all in the end?

Does beating one down
Control all his fears?

And provide safety for others
For the rest of their years?

I ponder these things
And I too have done wrong
And so I'm going to share
With you my very own song

It's a song of the soul
Where you get to know who you are
It's a rebirth and a hug
To the person you were

That little lost child
Who was so very afraid
Who bullied and cried
And hid in the shade

Who grew to hide
And used anger for protection
Which got him in trouble
And spread like an infection

Until one time he slipped
And crossed over the line
And now will pay for it
By doing his time

So we brush them off
And send them away
But we have not solved any problems
A life gone in a day

May feel good for revenge
But does nothing to aid
His soul or yours
Both of which God has made

So lets reach out
To those who are hurt
To those who are mean
Who kick up the dirt

Maybe time away
Will give them what they need
But let's just plant
One very crucial seed

Let's plant a tree
Of love and hope
For those who have hurt
And those who can't cope

They will come back
Either in this world or another
Remember that each one
Has a soul that's forever

You want it back
But it is gone
It's in the past
You must move on

I know what your thinking
How can this be?
And the story repeats
What your mind can see

What used to be
What once was
Your head won't let go
And that is because

Our minds rethink
And repeat
What seems off course
What was a mistreat

But don't you know
That is exactly right
What just happened
Both the dark and the light

You're trying to figure out
What went wrong
What should have been
That same old song

So turn your thoughts

Yes you can
You can change the way
And make a new plan

That starts today
Perhaps different than you thought
Get used to change
In this net you've been caught

No getting out
So now what to do
You can keep looking back
Or figure out who is you

Then when you're calm
And accepted your plot
You can climb out of the net
And see what you've got

A life to lead
Perhaps different than planned
But the one you had
Has been divinely banned

So pick up the pace
Today is your day
Your life starts now
Go find a new way

Go away stupid
thought
Who invited you here?
Bringing up the past
And the future with
fear

I knew in my head
Of course I should
But I was not aware
Of course I could

You were there
You silly self
Focused on taking
Right off the shelf

But now I know
And I am aware
And I am here
And I care

To be alive
To play, have fun
And that silly thought
Has gone on the run

It will come back
It always does
To bother me
And that's because

We let it, you know
Take over our minds
And where is our soul?
Lagging behind

So this is how
You become aware
But you must be brave
If you dare

You have to stop
And listen to how
You feel when you do
And be in the now

Then you must step
up
And the only matter
Is what you know now
Not the latter

Then don't say yes
When you mean no
And don't say no
When it's good to go

Listen inside
Not on the out
Listen and then
Give it a shout

It's Okay, it is
You can do this
I'll be cheering
Say it, who is

Strong and wise
Kind and smart
That's you my friend

Right down to your
heart

So I'll see you again
On the road you take
Further along
On the journey we
make

Pardon me, please
For the errors, I've wept
Lacking faith in One
Turning inward
Quiet I kept

Your pain I saw
With fear I led
My heart so hard
So now I beg

No longer am I
That girl you met
I now turn to you
My future you'll set

Forgive my transgressions
For the pain, the hurt
So long, times past
The guilt is worn

Forgive me
Pardon me
My bequest of thee
A heartfelt apology

A ship sailed away
today
And I did not get on
It was tempting and I
thought I might
But then it was gone

It's going to a life I
thought
Might be perfect for
me today
But I couldn't afford
its fare
And so I watched it
sail away

I got on this other
boat
It seemed better for
me now
But now I'm really
wondering
If that other ship
might be better
somehow

The one I'm on seems
a bit shaky

And what's really scary
you know
Is that I'm the captain
of this boat
And the one who
makes it go

To places where I've
never been
Much like the other
one
Except this is the one
I'm on
Sailing out unto the
sun

And rain and storms
and other adventures
I never know what I'll
see
On this ship that I
have titled
The Great Life of Me

Everyday we make a
choice
And some of those are
grand
And even the little
ones

And when we take a
stand

Those choices are all
boats you know
That sail out to the sea
And only one of them
Is the boat for you or
me

The other ones sail off
That we know for sure
But we're not on
those
No matter what the
lure

The one you've
chosen is yours
It's the life your living

It's the journey you
chose to take
It's the one for giving

You didn't get on the
others
So just let them sail
away
They're not for you to
live this time
This is where you'll
stay

On this boat that is
you
The one you're on
right now
This is you, this is
your life
So, live the best way
you know how

I wish I had
I wish I had not
I wish I was
I wish I was not

Why didn't I know?
But I think I did
Why was I so dumb?
An adult little kid

Why was I afraid?
Why was I scared?
Why couldn't I give?
Why didn't I share?

What was on that
screen?
What was so
important?
I lost so much
That I am certain

But here I sit
Pondering that
And missing now

Wearing the same ol'
hat

This wishing is dumb
Cuz I wasn't aware
Of all the benefit
Of taking the dare

It's not my way
To be bold and brave
I like to feel safe
Hold on and save

But then I wish
I had done more
Or spent more time
With you on the shore

So I'm here now
And this is what
matters
Yesterday's gone
Broken and shattered

Wish all you want

It won't make a
change
But living right now
Is right in your range

Take a deep breath
It's going to work out
Sing a little song
And give a big shout

To life, to love
To the here and now
Stand up for this
moment
You know how

Give that wish to
someone
Else who can use it
Help them out
You can do it

A wish of love
Means I'm thinking of
you
A wish of peace
Means I'm not so blue

This wishing thing
Is not so bad
It's starting to make
me
Feel kind of glad

So here's to you
I wish you much love
That you never look
back
And the light from
above

Shines on your day
Your family and you
And you live out each
day
Like a gift that's brand
new

I am only truth
And now I know
The fear that
Guided me once
And took over my soul
Allowed me to be
But not to live
I apologize to you
The way I am best
Writing it down
Now off my chest
Yet it sticks with
Me always
A mountain to climb
I pray you'll be waiting
Just give me
More time

Why do we hide?
I do not know
What are we afraid of?
Afraid to show

What if we tell?
What we really think?
Will we crumble?
Will we sink?

But we hide our
stories
We hide who we are
We hide amongst
those
Near and far

In their lives
Amongst our friends
We keep our secrets
Until the end

We lie, we cheat
We hide what's in our
cup
So no one will know
We drink it up

We swallow it down
And it sits and
ferments

Until one day it rises
All our energy spent

On keeping our secret
Way down inside
Now it's all out
Nowhere to hide

And we feel we're
ruined
We just can't go on
There's no way out
Can't sing our song

But it's OK that
you're here
Is simply enough
You are perfect no
matter
What you covered up

I understand
And I want you to
know
Your safe with me
With anything you
show

I feel you in my gut
And you're often on my mind
I've heard about you all my life
And you're often left behind

You help provide for me to live
On this place that we call home
We stash you, hoard you and then resent you
And for you we will search and roam

And honestly we worship you
Or at least give you more time than you deserve
And as our lives pass by
It's you we've come to serve

We spend hours of our days
Moving you around
And we'll leave family and friends for you
To go live in another town

Most times we don't even touch you
Or get to spend the time
And we feel either elated or depressed
No matter if we have millions or a dime

Some of us have so much
And it turns us into a witch
And some of us have so little
And we are truly rich

You are the idol we worship

Though you may not be made of stone
As we give you our attention
And when you're gone you'll hear us moan

But here's the thing we all forget
You don't get to go
With us when we leave this home
You stay right here and so

We need to give you less attention
I'm sorry but it's true
You do have value but not so much
And it's funny as we think you do

That expensive car is really fun
But it will go away
And the things that we don't need you for
Are the things that stay and stay

Time with a loved one or a stranger
Has more value than you
And acts of random kindness
Are worth millions and that is true

We've been taught to save for tomorrow
Which sometimes never comes
And even if it does
We use it to sit somewhere alone

But what if we just gave
Most of you away?

And lived just so simply
That would really pay

A package might not get delivered
With that very special thing
But what is all around us
Is something we can sing

About...with our family
And a special friend
No value on those we love
Who will be with us in the end

So here you go, go in peace
I'm glad you were here
But now my soul needs time for what is real
And those I love so dear

Heart beating
Buh beat
Buh beat
And then speeding
Buh beat buh beat
buh beat
When I'm
Thinking
Or waking me
When I'm
Sleeping
I'm glad your beating
But
I feel I'm
Sinking
As your beating

So hard
So fast
And then
You pause
And go again
But I know
You'll be here
Until the end
So please know
That you can
Go slow today
God's got this
Okay?
Easy pace
Not to fast
Unless we're climbing
And don't want to be
Last
Buh Beat
Buh Beat
That's better now
You can do this
Steady is how

Ah yes it's you again
The thing I do not
know
During the day you
disappear
And then at night you
show

You sneak up to say
hello
But you don't really
show yourself
You come as a dream,
a feeling or thought
The doorway into hell

Or heaven perhaps
It just depends on
how you appear
My mind is connected
somehow
And my actions and
my fear

You visit in the dark
Because you're afraid
of me
So you wait until I rest

To show what my eyes
cannot see

That everything I do
Has a result beyond
That every action I
take
Has effects that last
quite long

So I am sorry, If
I've ever let you down
And forgot you were
my friend
Always hanging
around

And watching my
every move
And holding me
accountable
And giving me a peek
To all good or
undesirable

And since you're
going to be
Accompanying me
perhaps forever
I suppose we should
get to know

One another as you're
quite clever

I'll try not to ignore
you
During the day when
you are silent
So that when you visit
at night

Our meeting will not
be so violent

So welcome and hello
To the backseat driver
in control
Thank you for the
signs and signals
For steering this gift,
my soul

"Someone" woke me
up
And I wish you'd go
away
I'm trying to numb my
brain
And you think you
can stay

Around my sleepy
mind when
I'm trying to sleep
And re-nourish my
body
The one I'd like to
keep

Healthy and happy
But here you are again
The unwelcome visitor
Waking me at 2 AM

Why can't you visit
When it's day outside
Then I'd be awake
But that's when you
hide

So now that I'm up
What is it you'd like
me to figure out?
What's disturbing my
soul?
I'm listening go ahead
and shout

But no, you just poke
me awake
And now I have to
think
About everything
that's bothering me
From my life to the
kitchen sink

Who betrayed me this
week?
And which child has
me worried?
Will I have a job to go
to?
Why is life so hurried?

Will there be a
tomorrow?
Will people have
water to drink?
And what about my
schedule?

My head is starting to
shrink?

Okay, I'm exhausted
now

That much you must
know
I'm sure someone else
needs a wake up call
Please don't tarry, now
you must go

Where are you soul?
I know you're here
But something feels
off
It feels like fear

Sometimes it wakes
me
Up you know
And I don't know
what to do
Or where to go

Those times when all
Seems right with me
I feel you close
And I can see

Like peanut butter
And jelly we are
Travelling with light
speed
Going so far

But then your quiet
cuz

I need to work and
sweat
On some parts of
myself
So you sit back while I
fret

My mind takes over
So there's no room for
you
So you just wait for
me
To do what I do

I know you're still
there
But everything feels so
wrong
My self, my brain
Singing that off-key
song

Then I must be quiet
And let you talk
We step out for a
while
And go for a walk

And you tell me to
breathe
Not to go so fast

And let life take its
course
Forget the future or
past

For now is where
I can meet up with
you
And we can walk
together
Like Robin and Pooh

For that's what Pooh
was

Robin's youthful
young soul
His best childhood
friend
Who would watch
him grow old

We all have a friend
Who will never leave
or hide
It's your very own soul
Sitting right by your
side

There's a place I often go when things get tough. It's behind a wall and I know it exists as I can see it from my side. My side of the wall where I live is busy with action and thought, but over there it's just white, pure and peaceful. So when I need to be just OK, I think "peace" and the space over on the other side comes to mind. One day a week, the Sabbath, the space opens wide and I can go visit, if I choose. I can stay here where there is thought and action, though the space on the other side is truly amazing. I've honestly not spent much time there as I'm working to feel safe enough to go, but I know it's there and it's calm and it's beautiful and it's just totally white. Like a Torah scroll, there are the letters of thought and action and then there is the hide, the white space that holds all the letters. We always think our thoughts and actions are the reality, but our reality is held up by the space and without it, there would be no reality. God created both the white space and this space of thought. He waits in the white space where we can visit and He holds us up as we go about our world of thought and action.

The light is gone
It's dark in here
And from where I am
I sense the fear

I'm scared you know
To just let this be
I feel alone
And cannot see

What if I just
Disappear
What if I cant?
Handle this fear

I can't just let it
Surround me so
There has to be more
Than this pain I know

Are you there God?
It's me you made
Why do you seem
So far away?

My tears are
All I feel on my face
My sadness is all
And it won't erase

I think I'll just wait
And learn to live
Inside of this place
It's all I can give

Patience that is
It's what is now
Waiting for you
To show me how

To see a glimpse
Of what tomorrow
may be
A small glimmer of
hope
To set me free

I'm getting used to
this space
In the dark where I
feel smothered
But now the dark
and I
Are used to each other

Cause it seems like
Were going to be
together for a while
And I found it likes
my frown
And not so much my
smile

But what it doesn't
know
Is that my hope is
strong
And every once in a
while
A gift comes along

A call from a friend
A voice that says I care
A text and email
A heart I can share

So maybe the dark
Is not so bad you see
Maybe the dark
Is the place chosen for
me

And maybe the joy
Will touch me one
day
Maybe I have to first
Find the light along
the way

Perhaps I have to
learn
How to live in the
dark
Perhaps you can visit
With your shining
bright spark

I lost my happy
Not sure where she went
Somewhere between
Should have been
And repent
She slipped away
One night as
I became aware
Of the fear
And manipulation
That took her somewhere
If you see her
Send her back to me
Let her know
She's missed
It's so hard to breathe
With out her
Making me smile
Happy come back
If just for a while

Embrace the dark
You were meant to be
Just let it sit
Surrounding me
For if you choose
To ignore its hold
You'll miss the message
The dark and the bold
From within this space
There is a light
But it only shines
Once you've seen the plight
Of a dark day
A sad tear
A heavy burden
A horrible year
It's then you can stand
And see the light
And choose to live
With God in your sight

Some days are dark
And the source I don't know
But it makes my heart race
And my stomach show
How it feels about
This new place called dark
How anxiety rolls
Through my body and heart
But then I realize
If I think of that space
In the wall I see
I can stop to be
It's an opening you see
And there is white space beyond
No one is there
But me and my song
God keeps the space
Available at all times
It's soft and it's sweet
And harm cannot find
This space I call Peace
This space I can be
This space that was created
For you and for me

So here it is
I'm really afraid
Cuz things just don't
seem
To be going as I
planned
And the truth is
I was getting a bit
Lazy with my life
And letting it go
Wherever it took me
And I'm the kind of
gal
Who lets things roll
And assumes it's all
good
To go
But I'm really scared
now
As nothing seems
right
And it's all stopped
And feels stale, stolen
and bare
So now I'm left with
Total insecurity
And well just me
Cause I don't have
anything
Else I can count on

Except God and He's
kind of hard
To read
And I also think
He's waiting for my
move
It's just I don't know
What that is
Right now
And why does
everything feel
So weird
Like I lost my grip
On what I knew
And the cash that flew
Now seems so few
So I think
I'll breathe
And just be
Until someone finds
The best of me
Because I know
She's here
She's just been abused
By the part of life
She could not use
In and out
Beat by beat
Live the now
It's the only way
It's the only how

This all knowing
Is not for me
Where does it go?
What can it be?
So afraid
What does it see?
Not now
I'm here
And this is me
Here on earth
I'm meant to be
I think
But that gnawing inside
Where is it from?
It wakens me up
So aware like the dawn
It knows I'm here
And I'm becoming aware
Of this something
That knows all
Of me

Behind my back
I didn't see
You coming with
A stab for me

Though you said
It was not intended to be
Your words ran deep
And far for all to see

And as the shock
Of my new reality set in
The life I had known now gone
The memory so thin

The world I had known
With love and joy
Was surely shaken
No more to enjoy

I wondered why?
So hostile so aggressive
Had your own pain been lying
Dormant and obsessive

So my gentle nature
Was all you needed
To hurt and destroy
Even though I pleaded

With you...To step back
To let us talk... to go slow
But your pain was too great
From long ago

We all have to learn
That our pain is not a weapon
That innocence is at risk
Justification is no reason

Because we are one
So what I feel you will come to know
So choose pain or joy
Either will show

Perhaps next time you will choose
Love as your weapon
And we can bask in the warmth
Of God's presence
from heaven

Hello integrity
So nice of you to stop by
Now I feel so darn horrible
So I stop and take that sigh

Was it the time I stole the other day
That made you pay a visit?
Or the lie I told about myself
Which one is it?

You're always so quiet
When I'm deciding what to do
But then you show up a bit too late
To tell me what I really knew

And all the reasons that I offer
Don't seem to matter a bit
You shake that big black finger
And I wallow in that pit

You're like that guest who's on the list
The one who shows up late
The one you think won't come at all
And then comes knocking on your gate

How about we make a deal
And you show up with the rest?
How about you stay with me
And all the other guests?

You know them all by name
Trust, Faith, Generosity and Love
They are friends of mine too
You all live in the apartment above

No need to lurk around
And hide out of sight
You're a welcome friend
So step out into the light

We can do this you and me
So don't hide in the shade
We can be best friends you know
And I don't need to be afraid

Of what others think
Or what they'll do
Or what they'll say
Because all that matters is you

You said you were a
friend of mine
You said you loved me
so
But when the
opportunity came
You gave me such a
blow

You went behind my
back
To do your dirty work
You hurt what was
mine to love
I think that makes you
the jerk

And now you wonder
why
You're left alone to
wonder
About why this
relationship ended
You need some time
to ponder

It's not that I don't
miss you
I always will and wish
you love

But some things must
be protected
It's ordained from
above

I don't stand to judge
you
As I myself have been
there too
When I betrayed
another
I can wear that shoe

So I know life goes on
But you must
understand
Betrayal will be
forgiven
But the trust is gone
and

I will go on living
without you
That my friend is a
must
I can choose to be
around those
Who support me,
whom I trust

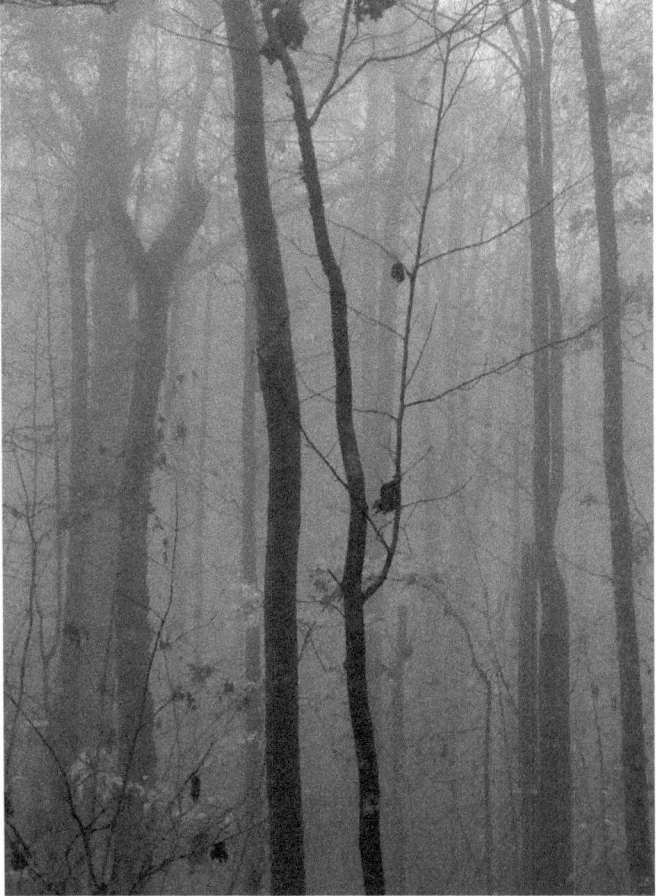

I wonder...
Never wounded
Never yelled at
Never neglected
Never criticized
Never ignored
Never despised
Never controlled
What existences do we change with each offense?
How much doing is halted?
Creativity stifled?
Memories faded?
Moments missed?
Souls squashed?
What purpose is there in feeding one ego at the price
of another's soul?
Can an ego hear a soul?

I spoke the other day
Words that were hiding
In my mind
Slipping out
For a brief moment
Getting something off my chest
And out of my head
I used my mouth
To tell a truth
From the way I see the world
But it was not mine to say
And so now I'm left
With the words gone
From my mind
But they left a hole
In my soul
For what I said
Was not so kind
And what I said
Really was not mine
To share
With someone
Else
And I can't undo
What I said
Just like you can't undo
What is done
It's just a hole
That left my head
And planted one
In yours
Instead

I came to visit today
I didn't know what to say
So I sat so quietly
And watched
So honestly
The wall I had formed
Would stay in place
I sometimes don't know
What happened
And why now
I am alone
I must mention
I seem OK
Yet inside
Everyday
I wonder
About the me
I used to be
I often
Feel quite sad
Alone
Though it is not so bad
I'm looking for signs
Of where I belong
And wondering
Where I should go

I see that you are happy
And so now I am confused
As your normal state of being
Is sad or mad, I'm bemused

And I was used to stern
I can ward it off
I have strategies I've learned
I'm used to a bit of scoff

I have my places to go
I have my places to hide
I know what to do
With Dr. Jekyll and Mrs. Hide

But this new person
Her I don't know
Why do I feel less comfortable now?
Who is that behind that glow?

Or maybe now I need
To ask myself and wonder
Who am I if only myself
When you were sad, I ponder?

Maybe now I'm here
A better place than where we started
I need to not only get to know the new you
But myself and what I wanted

Can I be the person you need?
Who is happy for you?
In every stage of your life?
And everything you do?

And can I be myself?
And grow into my soul?
Are you the one who can support me now?
As I grow from young to old?

Soulshine

"I grow silent. Dear soul, you speak." Rumi

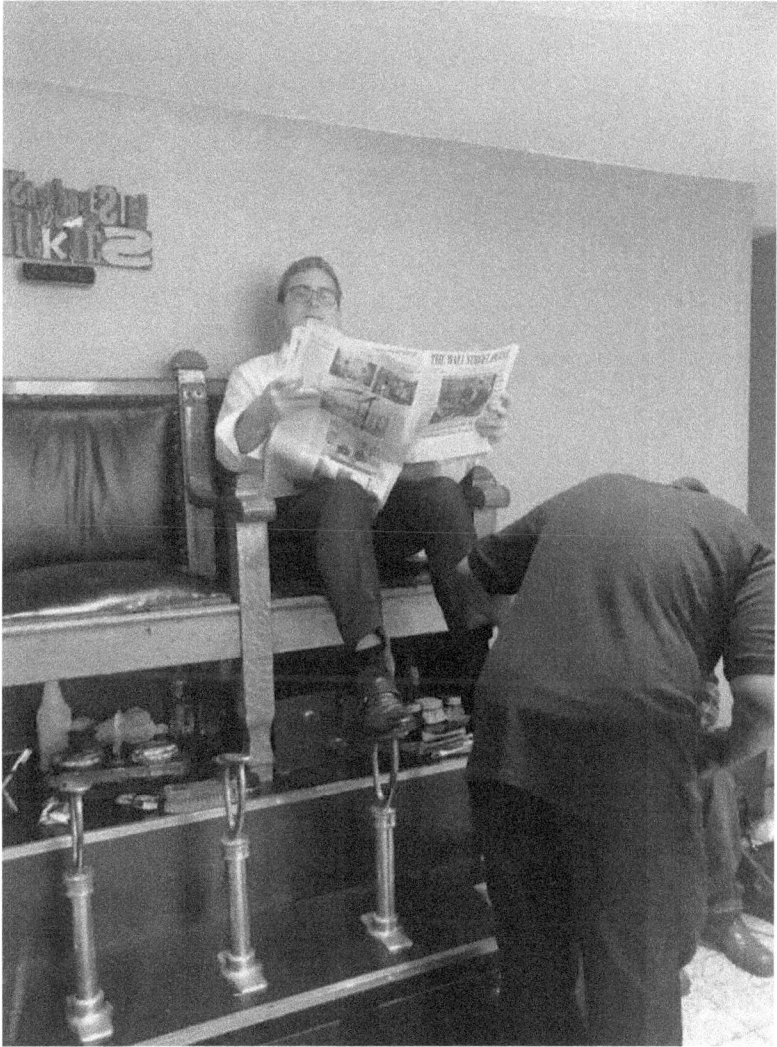

There is a little lake
It is mine
Though I know it is
not really
But I call it mine
My private place
My private space
A sanctuary
With no walls
I pray in that special
place
Just me
And birds
And trees
And the water calls us
all
To stop and wander
And wonder
And play
We see the reflection
Of those trees so tall
On a quiet morning
Unadulterated by it all
On a dock is me built
by my husband
On another dock is
the Heron
On another dock is
the plant
We are all witnesses to
our lake
While my dog sniffs
For rabbits

In the quiet
My children I see
Fishing, exploring
Boating and
swimming
And the ripples
Made by the fish or a
turtle below
Or a windy day
Or the leaves when
they fall
A rainy day is another
time
When the lake
Shows itself
Majestic and fine
Or a pristine night
When a light from a
home
Or above may shine
And a clear early
morning
The gawk of the geese
The song of the bird
We hear, we see
We smell this world
The wind on my face
As I walk with my dog
A moment in time
Thank you to
This little lake of mine
I will take you with me
So glorious
So fine

144

Every day I look at the lake and it is different.
Sometimes...
Bright
Misty
Foggy
Stormy
Windy
Rainy
Clear
...so you don't know it's even there.
Sometimes there's a film over the lake from leaves or
pollen.
And you wonder if it will be ok.
And sometimes the lake is moving from wind or life
living underneath or above.

But the lake itself always remains strong, steady and
living.

On a clear day one might not be sure which is real...
That which is above
Or the reflection below.
That which stands physically above the lake is
projected and reflected by the lake's surface.
It is the lake which gives the full beauty to that which
is above it.
What is your lake?
And what does your reflection show?

146

Butterfly
Where are you from?
So beautiful
You hover
With colors that say
I'm an amazing
creature
Enjoying this day
And you are not
ashamed
Of the new you
Who journeyed here
From where
You couldn't stay
As a caterpillar
You knew the signs
Said it was time to go
So you went inside
And waited so
Until your colors
Were ready to show
And now you spread
your
Love from flower to
flower
Such love you give
Through your nectar
It's like you always
knew
You had to be
More than everyone
Could see
Your were not meant
to
Crawl and just eat
worms
But to spread the light
And love and warmth
So when we know
We must go in
Though it may be
dark
And dim
In
In
In
In order to become
Who we are
To fly
So high
To reach
The sky
And share the love
Is not to die

I am a tree
A witness to a place
Where God kissed the earth
And the power of His kiss
Makes roots to grow
And reach so deep
And trunks to form
And branches to extend
And leaves to grow
Flower to bloom
And fruit to bear
Each kiss creates
A tree not like
Any other
Its attributes unique
And the gift of the kiss
Keeps giving long after
It has touched this earth
The tree is then the giver
Of sight, shade, fruit,
Flower, wood
And even in its
Death, the kiss keeps
Giving...to the soil
That nourished it
..to future trees
...to the earth
...and back to heaven again

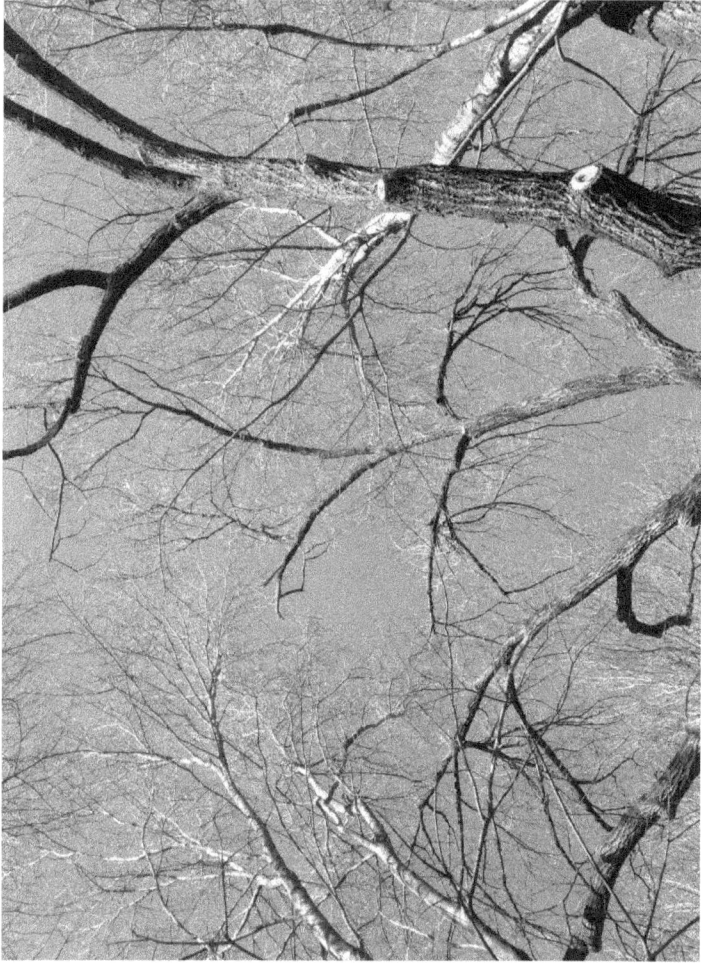

If you've ever looked
at a forest
And noticed just one
tree
And then followed
your eye
To a branch and then
one leaf

You'll see that it
stands out
And yet it also blends
in
And that is the beauty
of
A forest filled with
friends

Trees and plants and
shrubs
And animals that you
cannot see
And ones who peek
out
Just behind a tree

It is its own world
That bathes with
energy
Of love and life and
growth

Where a soul can
stand and be

The trees talk and
share
They even make a
change
And some live for oh
so long
And they cover such a
vast range

But no tree is angry or
hurt
Not jealous or mad
Only love for each
other
And they share what
they have

Every part of a tree
Will reach to water or
light
As both provide a
richness
For a spirit under
plight

Water brings
substance and
nourishment

And light brings
growth and love
And so we know that
every tree
Was planted from
above

So take a forest walk
Or find a single tree
And stop to just
breathe it in
Stop so you can be

There's a little leaf outside
Hanging on a tree
You were created
So that I can see

Holding on that branch
So incredibly tight
Though you seem so at ease
With your fate and plight

I see you
And you see me
In this moment of creation
Where we can be

Just two pieces of life
Noticing each other
Right now I see you
And no other

Tomorrow you may be here
Or maybe gone
Or maybe I
So let's sing our song

Of life that is
The one that you know
It's the song of your soul
A divinely inspired show

Falling down
Down
Down
Down
Running
Flowing
Spreading
Sinking
Clearing
Nourishing
And nothing
Will stand in
Your way
And life is hidden
On this rainy day
And it's

Quiet...

For a while
And then it's green
All around
Sounds of life
All surround
Waking up
To drink your gift
Like spirit food
You feed the
world
In every
Space

And it holds
You still
But then you
Rise
Up
And we wait
And we pray
Until
You come
Again
And
Again
For if you don't
Nothing can live
And if you do
We can also give
Water is life
Water is love
Descending
As a
Gift
From Above
Rain

You planted me
A Tree
Colors so clear
Branches that reach
To dance with the wind
Roots to drink
From knowledge within
Life that bore life
Your gift, mine
To nurture, your task
Mine, to ask
Differences learned
Respect to be earned
Seasons provide
A tree fully grown
And gratitude shown
For all that I am
For all I will be
I owe it to you
Mother of me

Fear can inhibit our ability to access our soul. Fear of others, fear of a circumstance. So we spend time looking for justifications. You become an accomplice to your emotions, fear and thoughts.

If we allow fear to make our choices as opposed to faith, we disconnect from our Source. I believe we have been conditioned to fear; whether we have learned this response from being surrounded by those who complain out of fear, who control out of fear, who need to be perfect out of fear or appease out of fear of rejection. Either way, we continue in this habitual pattern. When we let go of these responses and we look toward faith, we connect with God and we feel peace. We can then not be afraid to look inside ourselves where God awaits our meeting and not be afraid to surround ourselves by those who are different (ethnically, religiously, visually and so on). We are not afraid to be less than perfect and we have patience towards those who are not as quick as we are. We are not afraid of rejection or the journey. We can dance, sing, laugh and live without insult. We enjoy our mistakes and errors for we do not fear them. We enjoy each challenge for we do not fear it either. Fear is a disconnection from our Source.

But your soul is never afraid. It is uninhibited, honest and genuine. It lives without guilt, shame or disrespect. It is a guiding light in a dark hour and a small voice on a light day. And it has a direct connection to its SOURCE.

I heard someone
The other day
Speak of joy
And so I say

That what she said
Was joy is the color
That we bring to our day
And share with another

Joy is a rainbow and
It makes us smile
Like confetti or flowers
At least for a while

And we need these bits
Of color in our days
Simply because we are human
And those are our ways

And these colorful events
Like ice cream with sprinkles
Will keep us going
Like tie-dye with crinkles

It makes our mind
Want to live and create
And join in the fun
And participate

Though your joy may
Be a day on a lake

Mine may be sitting
With tea and cake

But joy makes us smile
Something we can share
Try to stay sad
That I dare

You, for joy is shared
With those we love
And I'd say that joy
Comes from above

So color your world
With blue, green and red
Whether it's your clothes, your office
Or a picture from your head

Paint a door pink
Wear a beautiful hat
Watch a hot air balloon
Get a swirly yoga mat

Color your life
Color your day
Toss out that black
This is the way

Of joy and smiles
Of laughter and fun
Grab that colorful kite
Get ready set run!

I think, we are like puppets and God is the puppeteer. We can move our own parts and control our own thoughts but the Puppeteer is always there if we need a thought. Some of us never give thought to our Puppeteer. Some of us do but never pull on our puppet strings and some of us pull every moment we can, and I think that makes the Puppeteer very happy.

Dear God
How are You?
Yes, it's me
And it's been a while
Because well I'm not
Good at talking
In God style
And though I know
You are powerful and
all
It seems like You have
A different style
Or maybe not
It's hard to tell
Do you like it when
I scream and
Yell?
Is it rules you want?
Should I step in line?
Or love from me?
Sometimes I feel tight
and confined
And quite confused
Which leaves me
In a state feeling quite
Bemused
And those tough
Parts of my life
Was that you?

Or were you just
Watching?
Waiting?
To see what I would
Do?
Do you know that I
am
So grateful?
For this life you've
Given me
That I can write this
Poem, laugh, breathe,
cry
And see?
Well, I am and also I
can't
Wait to be
The person who is just
Me
I know I'm not quite
there yet
Sometimes I just get
So upset
And sometimes I'm
scared
And wonder if
I'm making you proud
Or perhaps what I did
is not

Allowed
That time I lied and
cheated
Was one when I was
frightened
Of being alone
Or making someone
mad
Or sad
How silly it seems

Now that I'm here
But in this world
Full of blur
Things aren't always
So clear
So forgive me if
I've steered away
Please know I love you
Every day

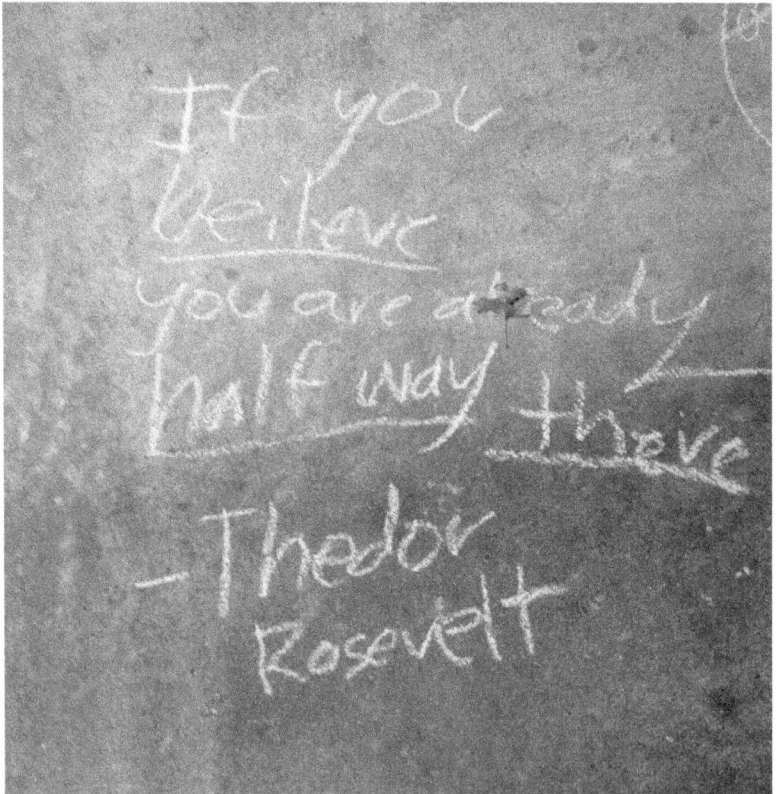

If you believe you are already half way there
— Thedor Rosevelt

What is belief?
How do we know it?
How come some have it?
and others don't show it?
Maybe a bit stronger than faith
But not as certain as knowing
Some "believers" are conditioned
Some beliefs bring a tale
But don't buy one
That comes with a quick sale
Belief takes time
To settle from the mind
To the heart
Often coming like a whisper
Sandwiched between
Wisdom
Learning
And eventually
Knowing

I like to write about God.
It's a bold task at the least.
Thoughts, perceptions and realities change day to
day.
Sometimes we are disconnected.
Perhaps God is love,
UNCONDTIONAL love.
It's very scary to put God onto paper like this.
It's almost like committing yourself to a certain
belief.
I believe God is accessible and always present.
I talk to God.
Sometimes.
I think he listens.
Always.
Sometimes I hang up too soon.
Shepherds talk to God.
God likes shepherds.
No sheep is left behind.
I don't often find God in a building,
But people in buildings like to talk about God.
Prayer comes from the heart.
Only the heart and through the lips, or art, or music,
or dance.
No one else can tell you how to feel about God
or even to feel at all.
Funny how everyone wants you to understand and
show you their God-
I think it's then that God is not around.

I am not sure that God and religion have a lot to do
with one another;
But they can.

I believe our intentions to make the physical more
spiritual has often turned out to making the spiritual
more physical.

People don't like to talk about God much.
It makes everyone a bit uncomfortable.

I believe that God resides wherever we wish to look.
If we are to know God then we must know one
another with the most soul searching, accepting, love
that we can give.

I thought I knew you
But maybe what I
knew
Was what I wanted to
see
And what I *thought*
was you

But that's Ok because
What I saw
Was what I needed
Not who you are

And that is what we
Tend to do
We portray our SELF
On what seems true

But if we get to
Know our soul
Then who you are
is clearly told

It means I'm aware
I can hear what's
unspoken
I can be fully present
For the whole *and* the
broken

Because a soul won't
judge
It accepts what is there
No fear or
explanations
For what is wrong or
fair

It speaks about love
It speaks about light
The seat of the soul
Doesn't understand
wrong and right

It's a song and a
dream
It's a wish full of color
The seat of the soul
Loves one and
another

Your cup runs over
Because the Source
has no limit
Your soul will never
run dry
Every day will fill it

Even when it seems
So tough and unfair

Your choice is your
soul
The soul is your chair

So take a seat

And sit for a while
Let your soul fill with
glory
Let your soul be your
light

Before there are
Rules
There must be
Love
Just as before there is
Design
There must be
Desire
This place or time
when
All is unformed
Is the basis for all
form
So a foundation of
Love
Is paramount for
Development
Otherwise the rules
and order

Lay on
The dark
The hidden
The shame
The chaos
But love knows none
of this
And creates a blanket
Of
Safety
Acceptance
Connection and
Growth
From which
A structure
A design
A person
Can grow
Love knows no
Judgment
Love knows
All

Love is a word we hear a lot
And its ambiguity seems to make it
One that is hard to grasp
We often use the word
To capture another's commitment
To ourselves
Hoping we will receive the word back
And there is the love we hand out
Through just goodness of our hearts
To others who come in and out of our lives
And there is a love that pours from within
Like no other feeling can exist
It is a love where we will sacrifice
All that we are for another to live
When you feel this love you know
Nothing can stop it from coming forth
Like a fire hydrant whose cap has popped off
And then perhaps there is a higher love
And that is a command to love God
As it is a directed love
That love is beyond our human
Understanding but one that we
Strive for everyday
Loving God with all your heart and all your soul

And I opened the gate to a garden and went in and
I was touched
I would not leave
But I could not stay
It was not for now
But a glimpse of tomorrow
Of another place
Another time
I find comfort in remembering the experience.
It is in our gardens where we have time to reflect
Where we can most intimately touch
And bear our souls
Where we must ultimately know ourselves
And where we're given hope

I think God is particularly disturbed when we compare ourselves and minimize ourselves to statistics. It must be something like having one of your children constantly trying to prove himself better than a brother or sister. It is hurtful to the parent. I do not presume to know what God wants; but I can say what God would not want: focus on minimizing others. For each of us to express Godliness through our unique selves and experiences, we must be kind-minded. I don't think any religious label has the corner stone on that market.

When I was a child I thought
That heaven must be grand
There had and I mean had to have
Swimming pools and beaches full of sand

And rainy days and trees
And sunny days with rainbows
And so many dogs to play with
This is what I did know

But then I grew to see
That those things were quite nice
But pleasure and joy and quite different
As so is heat and ice

But pleasure was what I knew
And it is what I sought
To find that something felt very wrong
As the goal was about me and not

Others who needed love and
Sacrifice to help me grow
So maybe heaven wasn't a place
But a way of thinking, you know

And perhaps yours and mine
Are not in all of the same
And maybe heaven has something to do
With integrity and the lack of shame

But what if we took a wrong turn?
Can we still get there I wonder?
Will heaven be waiting?
Sometimes this I ponder

I hope if I can touch your heart
And tell you that I care
I hope that door will open
If I love and if I share

So heaven is a thought
We should not call it a place
You get there when your actions are good
And shine upon your face

I hope to see you there one day
I hope we'll get to hug
And I really pray I see my dogs
And those I've come to love

I'm just a teaspoon of delicious here
From a large bowl of soup
Sitting in my spoon
Doing what I do

And you too came
From the very same spot
It's the only place to come from
Such a very large pot

It holds the entire universe
In its loving hands
This world and other worlds
All playing in one band

Like different instruments
We can play alone or together
A cacophony or orchestra
But the music goes on forever

And when your song is done
You'll go back to your spot
Your teaspoon of soup
Will be added to the pot

That soup is getting tasty
As the universe grows old
From all that we learn here
This idea may be quite bold

But you see it doesn't matter

How you look from your skin
Or what you practice
Because no one gets to win

This game of life is not
A competition or war
It's to spread your song around
And to be aware of others or

Your soup will get sour
And your music will be done
Because all of this only works
If we know we work as one

So play a tune with me
Let's make a song or track
So when we are done here
Our spoonful will not lack

Flavor, sweet as honey
Delicious to the soul
A spoonful of love
To be added to the bowl

I feel the change
Perhaps a new truth
It makes sense
It has direction
It feels safe
Liberated now by this new structure
I just wonder sometimes if God changes
How can something so infinite change?
How can something so infinite NOT change?

If you go somewhere that you believe brings you closer to God, yet you come back angry, then that place simply cannot be bringing people close to God. There are many stories of people who experience near death situations. I don't think I've ever heard of them waking up angry or irritated. In fact, they seem to embrace life with a newfound love and passion for people. I can't image anything closer in this world to God then "going to visit" the other side. So, if there are places on this earth, where people live with God, then surely those visiting would feel at peace.

Existing in planes
We know not
The soul...a visitor
Its chooser a body
For its task here on earth
In its most dense form
It exists here
Allowing the body, heart and mind
To steer
Free choice
Trusting itself to the physical world
Intending to make its owner proud

I have to make a
choice today
But my mind is a
swirling
I have to make a
decision now
But the thoughts keep
on twirling

I find myself frozen
As if doing nothing
will resolve
And while I'm stuck
out on this drift
Waiting for an answer
from above

But nothing is going
to change
Without direction
from me
And I can sit here and
think thoughts
From now until
eternity

So I'm going to have
to take a chance
And choose the best
for me

Or do Eenie Meenie
Minie Mo
To get me out of jail
free

Because being
paralyzed
By a decision I've had
in my head this long
Is like being frozen in
time
While the world goes
on and on

So I'm going to just go
for it
And ask God to help
He will be with me all
the way
Whether I fall,
succeed or yelp

I may make some
people mad
But they will move
along
I must embrace the
life I choose
That decision is never
wrong

The experience now long gone
Pushed behind
Yet it surfaces
Like air under water
At moments unexpected
The truth of it
Begs attention
Not so mundane
Unlike this world
It is meant for the next
The knowing of it
Much like the forbidden fruit
That provides too much
To handle just now
Yet our spirit yearns
For an explanation
The experience provides
And although so brief
That it must be
Time lain aside
All is meant to be
Heaven and earth

So let's journey on
To this place we do not know
A space where we can be
And we can grow

For staying still
Has cost too much
We lost our pace
Though we gained so much

Our hearts are healing
Our minds a swirl
But we are stronger and wiser
From the hurt we've endured

We will find a new sense
Of who we are now
We will remember the faces
Of those who showed us how

To be
To ask
To look beyond
With peace and open arms
Is how we will carry on

It seems as if our purpose here is not only to elevate the mundane, but also to elevate ourselves, an extension of God. The purpose of this elevation process is so innate that it cannot be fully understood and even often goes hidden.

But, I believe it is to the extent to which we elevate ourselves here that we will find ourselves when our time is up here. Our actions and thinking in this world will take us to a corresponding place in the next, so its seems.

So we must choose wisely, lest we become eternally mundane.

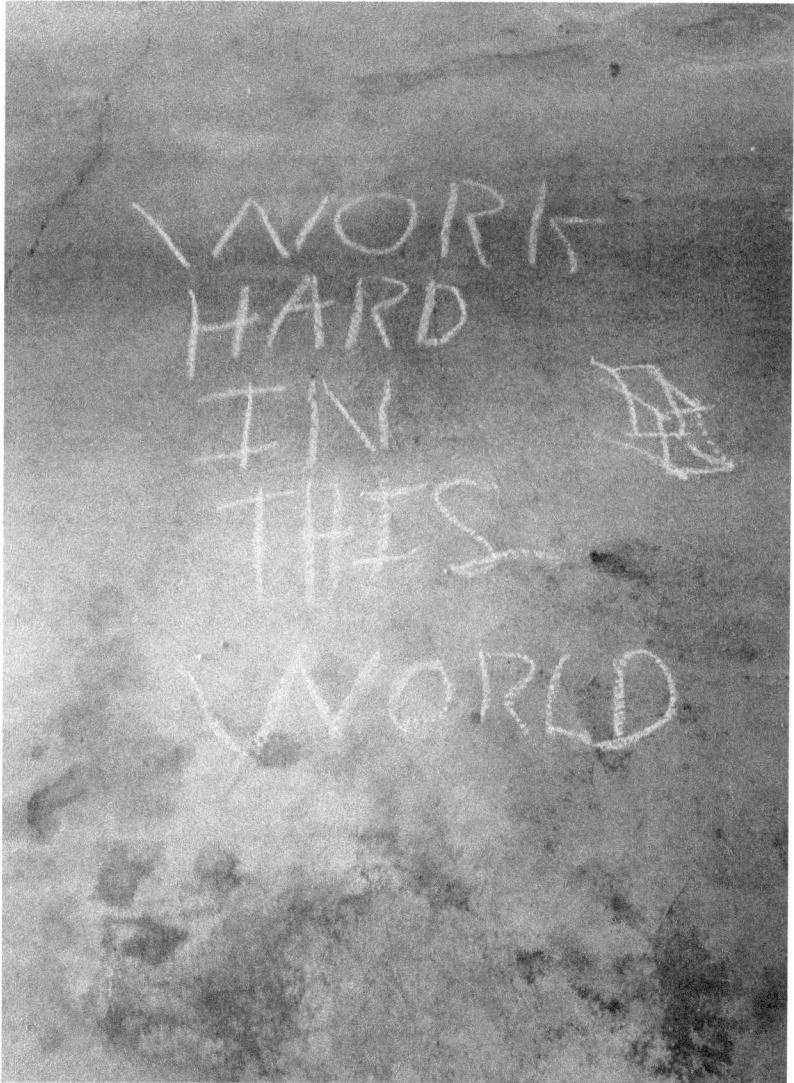

We need to stop the practice of pigeon holding people and labeling them. We do so for our own comfort, but in the end it prevents growth. It is comforting to set up boundaries, but it is spiritually awakening to remove them; and even more so never to put them in place, allowing the soul to drive the individual.

Did you know that feeling?
When everything seems right?
It's like all is amazing
And you can feel your light

And sometimes it's when
Things might not look so good
But you feel a love so strong
And you know that you should

Stop and just be present
And let your glory be your sign
Say thank you that you're here
We call that soulshine

It's your cup of grace and good
That helps you choose your best
That lets you lend a loving hand
You're no better than the rest

That you know and feel
A divine love that is so true
And helps you choose each day
What to say and do

Soulshine is like sunshine
But the light is deep inside
And when you feel like flying
It will take you for a ride

And on those rainy days
When your soul is hard to find
It's still there you know
So don't leave it far behind

You have to work really hard
To help it though those clouds
But I promise it's still there
Shouting really loud

There's a space I know
Though I avoid it much
You see I'm busy a lot
And don't have time to notice
The space where I can go
To laugh, cry or scream
To listen or to just be
But sometimes when I'm hurting
And the noise has gotten too much
The only place I can feel at peace
Is this space
It's quiet
Not even my thoughts are there
Just me
And it seems to be OK
With who I am
So we hang out for a bit
It's so peaceful there
And you can get there
Anytime you need to bare
Your soul or just to hang out
It's always there

I often wonder
What lies ahead?
What's on the other side?
What's over there?

And thankfully
It is not so hard
To find a bridge
To take us far

But more than what
Is visible to you
The bridge connects us
To a whole new view

So, the designing is crucial
Right up to the ridge
The materials of quality
To create the whole bridge

And as we look over
Those bridges we've crossed
We're thankful for all
No appreciation is lost

Enjoy each crossing
To a new point of view
Say goodbye to the past
And hello to a new you

Our purpose at hand
To seek out truth
Our tools
The sharing of our unbounded consciousness
We ask of your blessings.
Let our prayers ignite the universal plan, the good
within all existence,
And let us, we pray, be touched by the good.
Looking to You, Our Source, we join in spiritual
symphony
Let our prayers be heard

I'm worried God
If I'm doing Okay
You see I missed the
mark
The other day

I lost my temper
And I got mad
And then after that
I was just so sad

And now I'm worried
About the result I laid
On those I upset
And how they paid

And I know no deed
Goes undone
It all comes back
around
Everything under the
sun

And so my go-to
response
Is fear

And I often upset
those
I hold so dear

This fear I have
It runs around
And disconnects
everyone
Like the bad sheriff in
town

And it causes my own
Family and loved ones
To act the same way
To choose fear and
run

Such huge
ramifications
So much energy spent
On disconnecting and
protecting
It's like paying rent

On something gone
sour
Why do we do so?

192

Why don't we love
more?
I'm not sure though

I know that love
Heals and repairs
When we follow our
soul
It's like a beautiful
warm air

That hugs and pieces
The puzzle together
And each act can last
Just about forever

So we always have a
choice
Love or fear
Though down here we
forget
You see it's not so
clear

So we have to just
practice
It's much like a
muscle

Which ever we choose
gets stronger
And learns how to
hustle

So we can live in fear
Or we can live with
love
One tears down
And one builds up

One will line up
Our thoughts with our
soul
The other feels wrong
And makes us grow
old

I'm working on this
I really am
I can feel it already
I'm part of the plan

To connect and to
grow
To align with You
To put my soul in
high gear
To know what is true

Thank you sounds so silly
To say to the One
Who created all there is
Air, water and sun

But today I am free
And able to take a breath
Today I can go and be
I'll be thankful until my death

Today I can see
And there's music to my ears
I can take a walk with my dog
And live these many years

I can hold my husband's hand
And laugh with my child
Isn't life just glorious?
Isn't life just wild?

Oh yes, you say and remind me
Of all I cannot do
I won't deny what you say
For there's lacking that is true

But lacking never helps
One to live their life
Nope all that view of lack does
Is cause pain and strife

So what ever you get is yours
And you get what you get
And what you don't is not
So it's best just to let

Those thoughts go away
And replace them with a new view
One that's full of love
One that shows gratitude

So thank you for this moment
Tomorrow I don't know
But today I'm thankful for all that is
So up I am, let's go

Like a rock that hits you in the head
Life's lessons come to teach
What is needed to evolve yourself
And help your soul to reach

That place that only you can go
Set up for you to learn
What it means to live as a soul
Through every bump, hill, valley and turn

The experience you receive
May happen or caused by you
But how you respond to it
Determines each lesson that is due

It may be with a different person
Or a different time and place
But when you stop to think about it
You'll know you have the tools to solve this case

Whether you have love, loneliness, poverty or riches
Born Jewish, Christian, Muslim or not
Your life will teach you what you need
And those in your life help form the plot

As you the star of your very own show
The players: those on stage and in a seat
Don't think they are in the way
They were placed perfectly for you to meet

To push, to love, to help or hurt

Yes they are all part of the plan
The tragedies and the triumphs
Are all at your command

You can determine how this unfolds
And how you will react
You get to choose how you think
And how you interact

We come here with a mission you know
To bring love to this world
So set your intention to learn your lessons
Now simply let your soul unfurl

If every single moment
Was captured in a single glance
If every millisecond
Was given a second chance

Then we could have the time
To think our actions through
And see the outcome they may have
On everyone we knew

But we don't get a redo
To change the choices we make
So every single millisecond
Counts and it's a take

Pretend as if this is your show
And it's the only one we will see
Pretend as if this is your one chance
This moment is the one you will be

Known for, to the rest of the world
This moment is captured to show
Everyone, who you are
Everyone you know

So yes at this very second
And every one you live
You are showing who you are
How you spent each take and give

Is this the second you want recorded
To show the world who
You are when you are angry and mad
Sad or feeling blue?

You can feel what you feel
And express that with a swirl
But how you do so is who you are
It's your imprint on the world

Yes this very moment counts
Yes it matters now
So do it well, take stage right
And exit with a bow

Deep within
It speaks to me
No words, no sound
Just a part of me

An inside force
A spirit on high
An intuition, a feeling
A burning inside

Look for it not
In events that occur
It is simply your dealings
That causes it to stir

Your prayers not unheard
But is to ONE self that we speak
Pray intently from within
Lest the words make you weak

And do not be of many
Who separate themselves
From this most awesome entity
A true living hell

Your minutia annoying
It laughs at your days
When you stand in judgment
Out detailing each others ways

Yet it loves small moments
That lead up to great events
Living each day with a purpose
Every moment well spent

So bold to express?
Some of you in shock
You prefer to go on
Living behind your rock

I dare you to ask
What's my purpose in this life?
To get by, to ponder, to follow?
Or to spread goodwill outside?

Goodbye yesterday
I see you're gone
You saw me through
another day
And now it's dawn

Another day
will take your place
Another time
Will see my face

I hope its smooth
As you were not
But that's OK
I learned a lot

I'll take the lessons
I learned with you
And use them today
As I start anew

I never know
What might happen
each day
So I tread cautiously
But with hope I say

Bring it on baby!
I'm ready to roll
Cause yesterday taught
me
To set a new goal

So I say goodbye
yesterday
And hello to today
And tomorrow I'll
pray for
Another new day

Sitting, gazing, seeing them running
Yet I dare not move
The moments already gone
By myself, Yes
But alone, No
For my thoughts are always with me
I can't continue as was
For I must go out and draw my sword
Isn't that what we're supposed to do?
There's no time to sit and think
We must grab before it's all taken
Then why do I wait?
How do I know?
When the time is right?
To get up and go
Perhaps now is the time
To ready your heart
Hold onto your thoughts
It's now time to start

Journey on
Sight unseen
Destination unknown
So unpredictable

Turn within
Searching deep
Growing strong

Time to move on
The stirring begins
The discomfort

Ignoring the vision
It comes again
Back on the road

Until the journey
Ends

And so
I have so much more to say
But the pages
May just fade away

Though it seems
This journey is at its end
I think we know
It just began

A thought
Creates such energy
Our choices direct it
To hide or see

I have chosen to
Share mine with you
And now it is your turn
To share yours too

What makes you grow
Or makes you hide
What will you leave
When it's your time

My only advice
Be bold, Be kind
So the moments that pass
Connect with the Divine

About the Poet:

Greetings! I've been a poet since a young girl. I write as a form of expression, creativity, searching and prayer. I'm a spiritual seeker with a passion for great music, art and out of the box thinking.

I work by day as a physical therapist, blogger, and special needs and ergonomics industry consultant.

My love is thinking deep thoughts, creating, working with people, writing, hiking, yoga, spending time with my husband and family, and snuggling with my dog.

I am the author of A Tale of Two Souls, Joe's Market, Albert the Key Man, and now Songs of the Soul. I can be reached at kitov18@gmail.com. I look forward to hearing from you!

www.ingramcontent.com/pod-product-compliance
Lightning Source LLC
Chambersburg PA
CBHW051725040426
42447CB00008B/974